ECK WISDOM

on

Karma and
Reincarnation

ECK Wisdom

on

Karma and Reincarnation

HAROLD KLEMP

ECKANKAR

Minneapolis

www.Eckankar.org

ECK Wisdom on
Karma and Reincarnation

The terms ECKANKAR, ECK, EK, MAHANTA, SOUL TRAVEL, and VAIRAGI, among others, are trademarks of ECKANKAR, PO Box 2000, Chanhassen, MN 55317-2000 USA.   161218

Printed in USA

Photo of Sri Harold Klemp (page 88)
by Art Galbraith

Second edition—2017

Library of Congress Cataloging-in-Publication Data

Names: Klemp, Harold, author.
Title: ECK wisdom on karma and reincarnation / Harold Klemp.
Other titles: Spiritual wisdom on karma and reincarnation
Description: Second Edition. | Minneapolis : Eckankar, 2017. | Rev. ed. of: Spiritual wisdom on karma and reincarnation. c2010.
Identifiers: LCCN 2017019883 | ISBN 9781570434488 (pbk. : alk. paper)
Subjects: LCSH: Karma. | Reincarnation--Eckankar (Organization) | Eckankar (Organization)
Classification: LCC BP605.E3 K574453 2017 | DDC 202/.2--dc23
LC record available at https://lccn.loc.gov/2017019883

♾ This paper meets the requirements of ANSI/NISO Z39.48-1992 (Permanence of Paper).

CONTENTS

YOU ARE SOUL

$\mathcal{Y}$ou are Soul, an immortal being created in the timeless worlds. You existed before birth and endure beyond time and space. God made Soul before the worlds of time and space began.

Soul comes to earth from the higher spiritual worlds to add to Its experiences. It inherits many lifetimes for the chance to learn.

And learn It must.

KARMA DISHES BACK WHAT WE DISH OUT

*W*hile shopping at a grocery store, my wife, Joan, and I saw three skateboarders outside. They were dashing here and there in the traffic, not paying a whole lot of attention.

Management saw the skateboarders were putting the store's customers at risk and sent an employee to nicely ask them not to skateboard there. As the woman turned to go back into the store, the leader of the skateboarders looked around and, almost with a sneer, said, "So, what's she going to do to us?"

The very next instant, his hands flew

up in the air and he fell flat on his brains—yes, on his seat. Unfortunately, the helmet was on his head.

Of course he jumped up quick as a whip and dusted himself off. Very embarrassed his buddies should see his downfall like that, he hopped on his skateboard and scooted off.

Well, the blessing is he didn't hurt his brains. And the lesson was, for us maybe, karma is of our own doing. So when he went flip-flopping all over like a fish out of water, he was just paying himself back real quick.

You can call it the Law of Karma, the Law of Cause and Effect, as if it's some great law that works rather arbitrarily. But it doesn't.

For the most part, on the daily karma level it dishes back what we dish out. If you dish out ice cream, you get ice cream back. And if you dish out some bitter, bitter drink, well that's what you get back.

Karma may jump in there and balance the books for you right then. Or it may take its time because it sees you're wearing padding. So it'll wait a little while, until you're more exposed, and then get you.

Yes, there is good karma.

When we say about someone, "It's his karma," the understanding often is it's bad karma. That karma is bad, always bad. But it isn't at all.

If we see someone who's enjoying the fruits of doing well in some arena of his life, the usual reaction is, "Some people are born with all the luck." Jealousy and envy creep right in. But if somebody is having a hard time, we say, "He got what he deserved. It's his karma."

So whether you're good or whether you're bad, you can't win if you've got a critic who doesn't have a good spiritual understanding of himself.

4

WHY PEOPLE ARE UNHAPPY

*W*hat do you suppose makes people unhappy? A survey would probably list a hundred reasons, both real and imagined.

Now how many of those people do you think would like to hear the true reason for their unhappiness? Just a guess—very few.

The choices you've made in the past are the direct cause of all your unhappiness today.

If this answer doesn't suit you, don't read another word. You have better things to do. But maybe you're one of the few people who doesn't absolutely reject the above explanation for your unhappiness. Then keep reading. Perhaps you'll see *how* and *why* individuals make bad choices.

Most important, you may learn how to stop making them.

How We Get Here

Soul enters this world to pursue a series of tasks, for each is an exercise in spiritual purification. Taken as a whole, these assignments make up one's destiny. To set the tone for Its mission, Soul enters a new lifetime with a body of strength or weakness, of great intellect or a simple mind, in a popular shade of skin or not, either as a male or a female, into wealth or poverty.

The idea of destiny as a concept is out of fashion in much of today's Western society. People want to be captains of their own lives. They wish to run their own fate. They will shape their own tomorrows. Yet how can they do so without a knowledge of and an appreciation for the meticulous Law of Karma?

Or especially, of the Law of Love?

In spite of all fictions about who is the

master of their own fate, they cannot even set the conditions of their birth. So the rules of karma and reincarnation remain a mystery, and they find a great deal of sorrow and disappointment in the outcome of their plans.

How could the stiff rules of karma include them?

Many would like to think they don't, sure of being above the common pool of humanity and thus exempt from these rules.

The Lords of Karma

By and large, though, the Lords of Karma—not the individual—select a family for each Soul. They are responsible for the distribution of karma from the time each Soul first enters this world.

The Lord of Karma is like a minor's guardian. He administers a trust on behalf of a spiritual infant, arranging for him or her to join a family with the best prospect for that Soul's unfoldment. In selecting the time and place of reincarnation, the Lord of Karma is the sole judge. He is the sole arbiter in the choice of a body, health, family, or future. The Lord of Karma alone sets the conditions of most people's fate.

Placement is a simple karmic detail. The Law of Karma governs all such placements, and he is only its agent.

The primal seed for each incarnation exists under the umbrella of destiny, which we also call past-life karma. On a practical level, genetic, cultural, and social elements combine to decide Soul's place in this world. For people on the lower end of the survival scale, the Lord of Karma alone chooses the time and place of rebirth.

Soul Follows the Script

Soul then follows the script of destiny and enters a physical body.

After birth, the name of the game is survival. The survival scale, by definition, is a measure of one's can-do instincts.

But karmic placement does set other standards for individuals on the high end of the spiritual scale. More of them enjoy a voice in the choice of a human body or place of birth. They sense the need for spiritual freedom, a view gained from many past lives, and the self-responsibility that goes along with the package. So these Souls demonstrate creative ideas and inventiveness in their incarnations. For the most part they are cheerful, upbeat people.

Spiritual gains in past lives have given them a voice in choosing some of the conditions in their present incarnation.

They have earned the right.

Think of destiny as the equipment, talents, or gifts that one brings to this life. They carry a divine mandate to use them for the good of all life. It's our responsibility to do so, with wisdom.

The idea of destiny, or fate, is poked fun at in many Western circles. Yet it is an age-old principle of the spiritual life.

What is the basis for a cultural bias against fate?

People are in a state of confusion about it. They wonder, *How can fate and free will exist side by side?* Destiny controls the conditions at birth. Much of what an individual does after birth is an open book, an exercise in free will.

To sum up, fate governs the conditions at birth; free will allows a choice as to how to move beyond them.

Free will can offset or even overcome the drawbacks of destiny, but only through the awakening of one's consciousness. One may thus reshape both his material and spiritual life.

FAMILY KARMIC TIES

*P*eople wonder how they get into the families they get into.

It's always the Lords of Karma who make the final decision between lifetimes. Or, if you are ready for the path of ECK, the Inner Master and the Lords of Karma decide together which setting, which group of people from your past would be best for you to join as a family, so that you can have the best spiritual opportunity in this lifetime.

The best spiritual opportunity is not necessarily the easiest life.

I think many of you will agree that your life has been anything but easy. In fact for many it has been very hard. Sometimes the best way to learn the spiritual lessons is through a life of hardship.

I had my hardships when I was growing up. I have my hardships today. Life will either crush you, or you will rise above life, to live more fully and with more joy.

Family Karmic Groups

When my daughter was preschool age, she said to me, "Do you remember when we were in Sweden and I was your mother?"

Children are always telling their parents what they know from past lives. But if the parents come from a religious background, Christian or any other, that does not teach the principle of reincarnation, they are not equipped to understand what the child is telling them.

"I remember very well," I said. "I also remember another time, more than a century ago, when I was a French soldier taking part in the Napoleonic blunder in Russia. I was wounded and needed help, and you were my nurse."

How easy it is to dismiss a past-life story with, "Just another dreamer's tall tale." And it's a real temptation to discredit young children who give detailed accounts of past lifetimes. Even if it means ignoring the candid descriptions of settings, situations, and possible family ties of old. Yet this happens all the time in families with children up to five or six years of age.

It's hard for some people in a Christian society to accept this information about reincarnation as a foundation for the miracle of birth. So they make up other explanations, that past-life claims are maybe some kind of mental transference.

Divine Love in Action

But wouldn't it be less of a problem to accept the simple fact of rebirth? Then you'd find sense behind the bounds of reincarnation.

13

Genius and disability are two quick examples of the influence of past lives.

People of religions other than Eckankar know and accept the principle of reincarnation: It's a principle of divine love in action.

Reincarnation allows people, like you and me, to have a chance to develop the quality of divine love. This opportunity comes through the hardships and uncertainties of life, as well as in the joys and fulfillment of living.

Thus we develop the quality of divine love. This love makes us more godlike beings.

SATISFYING YOUR
PAST-LIFE CURIOSITY

A group of students from Ghana traveled to another country for a year's study. They wanted to become more fluent in French.

One of the girls, a black student I'll call Mary, happened to meet a white German man. Soon they were close friends. Her acquaintances started to talk.

"Got a romance going?" they asked. "With a whitey?"

When someone of a different race, nationality, or even habits breaches the established order of a community, many times it's a recipe for trouble. Eyebrows are raised, and fair-weather friends run up their true colors. So her friends began to spread rumors and pass falsehoods about her friendship with this white German male.

Mary wished to lose neither her friends from Ghana nor her new white companion. She debated about the best course to take. To soothe the ferment, she sought counsel in a spiritual exercise.

An Easy Spiritual Exercise

It's easy to do a spiritual exercise. Shut your eyes and imagine a conversation with your spiritual guide, whomever you feel comfortable sharing the secrets of your heart with. It can be Jesus or some other religious figure. ECKists look to the Mahanta, the Living ECK Master, the spiritual leader of Eckankar.

So in a spiritual exercise, Mary said, "Please, Mahanta, give me an insight into this. What can I do? I don't want to lose my friends on this side or my friend on that side."

Such was the concern she laid before the Mahanta.

In the next instant she became aware of being in a past lifetime, standing on a shore with a baby in her arms. Close offshore stood a slaving ship. White men dotted the beach. They brandished whips at a line of black slaves ranged along the sand, shackled in chains.

They herded blacks onto the ships while she watched in tears, with a child at her breast. Her husband was one of the slaves. She begged the slave masters, "Please let my husband go. We have a child." Her plea brought harsh laughter.

Soon the last line of slaves boarded the ship. As they embarked, her husband cried out, "If we don't meet again in this lifetime, surely we will meet in another."

So Mary realized it wasn't mere chance to have met this white German student and developed such a strong attraction for him. It was a past-life connection. She also began to notice an oddity. Whenever he was with her, he behaved like an African. He walked, talked, and gestured like an African.

She used to observe him and wonder, *Now where did he pick that up?*

When this inner experience had ended, the Mahanta said to her, "Your friend in this lifetime was indeed your husband then."

Finally, Mary understood the strong rapport between them.

The Great Leveler

After this she could better handle the faultfinding of her friends, who tried to intimidate her by saying, "You shouldn't be seen with that white man. What will people think?"

This criticism was the voice of the social consciousness speaking. It's an element of the human state that tries to put everybody within a society at the same level. It abhors a taller head in the crowd and attempts to pound all heads to the same social, financial, or philosophical level. This social consciousness is the great leveler. Its spiritual harm comes in its frantic zeal to stamp out individuality.

After this inner experience Mary drew a firm line with her friends, because now she knew the origin of her affinity for the white German. He was a dear friend from the past. And there she took a stand.

Past Lives Are Tied to Karma

The Law of Cause and Effect, or the Law of Karma, is always in play your whole life. You must know how to live in harmony with its exacting terms. The experiences that derive from an adolescent or mature understanding of that law will, in time, bring you to an acceptance of divine love.

That's the reason you're here.

Sometimes people ask, "What does Eckankar have to offer that's unique? How is it different from Christianity?" So I may speak to them of karma and reincarnation.

And karma and reincarnation are not just for Souls in human form.

Tiger Lily Returns

When a woman I'll call Kerry was thirteen, she moved to a new town with her family, and she was lonesome. One day, she was with her mother, sitting in front of a store on some bags of fertilizer. Her father was inside the store paying for supplies. As Kerry and her mother were sitting there, all of a sudden they saw something moving behind the bags of fertilizer.

It was a little kitten. It seemed lost, so Kerry put it inside her shirt and carried it home.

When they got home, she showed the cat to Dad. He wasn't real happy, but he said, "All right, you can keep it."

This cat was a companion for her for almost twenty years. They were together until she turned thirty-two.

Kerry had found that the longer they were together, the more she loved the cat. Her love for the cat grew deeper and deeper. And about that time, she read one of the stories in the *Eckankar Journal*, an annual magazine with stories by members of Eckankar. The story told of a cat owner whose cat had reincarnated to be back with her.

Kerry knew it was getting near to the end of the cat's life. So she began telling her cat, "Tiger Lily, if you ever want to come back, please come back. Because I love you."

Finally it was time for Tiger Lily to go. She had spent many good years of happiness, love, and service on this earth.

For two and a half years after the cat was gone, Kerry wondered, *If Tiger Lily ever comes back, how will I recognize her?*

How Would She Recognize Her Friend?

How would she be able to recognize her dear friend Tiger Lily?

About this time she got married to a wonderful man. And this man had a wonderful dog. Unfortunately the dog liked to chase cats. Now she worried, *If Tiger Lily comes back, how will things work out with the dog?*

One night Kerry had a dream. In the dream she suddenly knew that Tiger Lily was back. When she woke up, she said, "I know Tiger Lily's back now. I'd better talk to the dog and see what the dog feels about this. How would the dog like a cat here?"

So she began talking with the dog. "How would you like a cat?" she asked. The dog wagged his tail. She took it as a good sign.

Kerry began to notice people giving away kittens. Each time she saw this, she wondered, *How am I going to know? Is that the kitten? Is that Tiger Lily?* Finally she said to the Mahanta, "I don't think I'll be able to figure this out with my head. I'm just going to have to trust my heart."

One day, she was over at her husband's parents' place, and they had just had dinner. The couple was ready to leave when a young kitten came running down the street.

Cats are very nonchalant about things like reincarnation. "There's my owner," the cat probably said as she came running up to the woman. "I've been waiting for you." Kerry looked at the kitten. It didn't look like Tiger Lily, but she picked it up.

The kitten immediately licked her on the nose and began purring. Kerry's head was spinning. She had waited two and a half years. She had wondered, *How will I know? I don't want to get the wrong cat. I want to get Tiger Lily.* And here was this kitten, so glad to see her, licking her nose and purring.

Her mother-in-law said, "I know where that cat belongs. It lives down the street. We'll go ask the family if you can have it."

"No, no," Kerry stammered. "I don't know."

But the mother-in-law said, "Come on. We'll go over there." So she dragged Kerry over to the neighbors. "Go on and ask them," she said.

Kerry still couldn't talk. She was stammering, unable to get any words out.

Her mother-in-law said, "Could she have this kitten?"

The neighbors said, "Sure. And if it doesn't work out, just bring the kitten back."

There were problems at first. The dog did like to chase the cat, so they had to work with the dog. And the kitten hadn't been completely house trained, so there were messes on the rugs. But each time Kerry looked into the cat's eyes, she could see it was Tiger Lily. There was no question. Her old friend had come back.

You've Lived Before, and You Will Live Again

$\mathcal{T}$he great benefit of the ECK teachings is that they offer spiritual freedom.

Each religion holds out some promise to its followers. The word of Christianity to its people is the redemption of sins, a problem that stems from Adam and Eve, who disobeyed God in the Garden of Eden. Yet for their error, all future generations should carry the blame. A Christian, lost spiritually at birth, has the stigma of this original sin automatically fastened to him. Original sin means inborn guilt.

By contrast, the ECK teachings speak not of guilt but of responsibility. People are where they have put themselves.

How Karma and Reincarnation Lead to Spiritual Freedom

The theory of one lifetime per person is an example of an immature theology, for it does not account for the fact of reincarnation and karma. These two parts of the ECK teachings put the responsibility of a person's life directly where it belongs—upon the individual.

All people make their own world.

Where does spiritual freedom fit into the ECK teachings? God has placed each Soul upon earth to gain the spiritual purity and experience It needs to become a Co-worker with God. From the very beginning, many lifetimes ago, Soul made blunders. It was like an infant first having to find out how to crawl, then walk, while learning its place in the family and society.

Growth and development are a natural part of the divine order.

The ECK teachings say that people create karma, a debt with Divine Spirit, by ignorance of divine law. Time and experience will teach them better. However, it usually takes lifetimes to work off primary, daily, and reserve karma, because people forget their divine nature.

This forgetfulness shows up in anger, vanity, greed, and other harmful traits. The result is more karma.

For that reason, we speak of the wheel of karma and reincarnation. More karma brings on more lifetimes. However fast people run, they must go even faster to stay ahead of their deeds, which threaten to catch and swallow them. Is there no end to this cycle?

Soul's Wake-Up Call

There surely is. After an individual has passed so many lives in one religion or another, been whipped this way and that by life, it eventually dawns on him there is no way to beat the game alone. All running gets him is more running.

At this point, a change occurs, perhaps as spiritual doubt. Or maybe it's a vision. A large percentage of people in the United States claim at least one vision, a strong and unforgettable dream, or an out-of-body experience. That experience is a wake-up call from the Mahanta, the Living ECK Master.

From that moment on, they become the seekers.

Yet they may spend the rest of this life in the church of their youth, too scared to leave it for a path like ECK, which gives them more satisfying answers.

They are still the seekers. Perhaps in the next lifetime they will find the courage to say, "What am I doing here? What is the meaning of life?"

Eckankar can show all people the most direct route home to God. Yes, there is a quicker exit from the wheel of karma and reincarnation, but most people will settle for a longer, more difficult way home.

What about spiritual freedom?

It is Soul's final release from the Law of Karma and reincarnation. The ECK teachings say that to live a karmaless life, one must do everything in the name of God.

At first, the Dream Master is the teacher. This teacher is the dream form of the Mahanta, the Living ECK Master. God has given him the spiritual power to act as both the Inner and Outer Master for those who want a more direct way out of these lower worlds. A guide and wayshower, he carries the key to the Light and Sound of God, two necessary parts of divine love.

The Path of Truth Starts in the Heart

Love is the force that returns Soul to God. For the path of truth starts in the heart, and the journey home to God begins with meeting the Mahanta in either a dream or in person. The Spiritual Exercises of ECK give strength and comfort, for these simple daily contemplations give one a stronger bond with the Divine Being. We call the path of ECK the Easy Way.

So the main benefit of ECK is spiritual freedom.

The entire aim of life is to find that freedom. Though the earth may shake and tremble, the person who loves God above all else will endure with peace of heart and mind.

MAKING LIFE BETTER WITH AN UNDERSTANDING OF KARMA

A past life was a moving force in teaching you compassion for others, even if in that life you might have showed no empathy for the suffering of others. At times, perhaps, you played the role of torturer, cruel lord, or even terrorist. A later life, then, to restore balance to the karmic scale, demanded you suffer the indignities of a victim. So you became the tortured, the oppressed, and the violated.

It's all in the game.

Each lifetime teaches at least one lesson and often dozens.

Of course, other lifetimes were routine

ones. With no monumental lessons, they nonetheless served as an opportunity for healing and reflection. You may have jockeyed from an early lifetime of adventure to a later one of rest. People do return to earth to heal. They squirrel away in a quiet place in some pastoral setting, a token reminder of the heaven they left behind.

Learning about Ourselves

During my first years in ECK, I had the good fortune to experience many past-life recalls. Some were pleasant. There were also a number of unpleasant ones, recalls of lost opportunities in reaching some desired goal. Not memories to celebrate in the least.

Yet each lifetime, even a supposed failure, gives a fuller understanding about your spiritual nature. You learn about yourself as a spiritual being.

Soul is immortal. It has no beginning or end. It (you) exists because of God's love for It, which is the whole philosophy of

Eckankar in a nutshell. Our mistakes in this and past lifetimes are the polishings of a precious gem in the rough.

Some years ago on my first visit to Paris, I roamed this fabled city that remains the glamorous belle of Europe. Paris had been my town on more than one occasion in recent incarnations. The last major lifetime there, the one I shared with my daughter, was during Napoleon's ill-fated march on Moscow in 1812.

Napoleon had marshaled six hundred thousand troops and crossed the Russian border in June, but by October the Russians had forced his retreat in the biting cold of winter. Only fifty thousand French soldiers escaped the Russian regulars. The rest died.

Along with other young men of France, I had been compelled to leave wife and home for war. There was no choice in the matter. All able-bodied men received orders to join Napoleon's vast military forces.

The march into Russia began in the summertime, but we saw little of the enemy—except for the major battle at Borodino in September. It was a phantom force that liked to slip away before a major face-to-face encounter.

All through history, the Russian winters have proved a stout ally to the Russian people. Hitler, the reincarnation of Napoleon, tested his luck again in World War II with the same disastrous results. His armies suffered a rout as convincing as did those of Napoleon in the earlier campaign.

In late autumn, I fell to a grave illness outside Moscow during the ragged retreat of the French army. Here my last days in that lifetime were attended to by a young Russian woman whose family tried folk remedies to restore me from a bout with pneumonia. In this life she is my daughter. All attempts at recovery, though, failed as frostbite ate at what little health remained.

Napoleon had underestimated the enormity of supplying his large army with food and clothing.

As a consequence I left that life a disillusioned man. His shortsighted plans were at the root of our bad luck. They caused my untimely passing. Our summer uniforms, in tatters after the harsh summer campaign, were a thin joke to the Russian bear of winter.

I brought two strong feelings into this life from that period in the early nineteenth century. One is a distaste for cold weather. The other, a respect for leaders who draw up careful plans before launching big projects.

Character Building

Many people do not know the fact of Soul's rebirth into a succession of lives on earth. Few learn to recall past-life memories so that lessons of long ago can be recaptured for advantage today.

Most run their lives as if this stay were a one-shot deal—the beginning and end of all that's worthy of reflection. Yet is it a crime to say that Soul inhabits a physical body but one time? Or that It never chafed under a master's discipline in a past life? Or that It never took on other incarnations at the death of those bodies, to see rebirth today and advance Its spiritual education?

No, it's not a crime to be ignorant of divine law. Experience is a hard-nosed teacher; time, the great educator.

Our character is made up of virtues and shortcomings, and all are a development from past lives. A reason lurks in the background of every twist of personality. Each trauma from a forgotten life shapes our conduct in a given way. Without exception.

Unless, of course, the force of Divine Spirit enters our consciousness to override the mind's knee-jerk reaction to life's challenges.

Divine law is the beginning and end of all truth. That law includes karma and reincarnation.

GRADUATING FROM THE WHEEL OF REINCARNATION

There are more people in the world who have an understanding of reincarnation and karma than do not. This may be a shock to a Christian society that believes in one life here and the rest of eternity there.

But some of you know in your heart, and do not just believe, that there is something more to the scheme of life.

All People We Meet Have Something to Teach Us

A man I'll call Bennett, for his privacy, grew up in Africa, lived in Europe for a bit, then came to the United States. When he was living in New York City, he was very disappointed with American women. He thought they were shallow—probably because he wasn't getting anywhere with them.

One day, while talking to a friend, he said, "How could anybody want to become friends with an American woman? They have nothing to offer." And his friend said, "All people we meet have something to teach us, if we would but learn."

Bennett thought about this for quite a while, and he accepted it. He realized that all the people around us are here to teach us something. That often we come from a certain culture with certain trappings, certain beliefs, certain taboos—and we bring all our baggage with us when we go to another country. And we expect everybody there to do things the way we do.

So, when Bennett's friend said we can learn from other people, even American women, it made a point with Bennett. He stopped looking at the problem, and he's now looking for a solution. And this is a big thing.

He learned that instead of judging another person, just to accept him or her and try to understand the lesson that life is trying to teach through this person.

The Great Ledger Book

If you grow up in a family with a lot of kids, and you get to hitting each other, a parent comes along and tries to separate you and find out who's at fault. You point a finger and say, "He started it." And, of course, that works until your brother points back and says, "I did not. He started it." And then it starts all over again.

Well, that's what happens lifetime after lifetime too. In this life we rub someone the wrong way, they rub us the wrong way. To us, it doesn't seem important what rubs someone else wrong. What's important is what rubs *us* wrong.

That's one part of karma. The other part is where everything is kind, harmonious, smooth, and good. That also counts up in the great ledger book.

When the accounting is done after this lifetime, the Lords of Karma look in the ledger and say, "Hmmm, let's see. He's going back for another lifetime because he hasn't learned how to get off the wheel of reincarnation. But his ledger says he's done pretty good this lifetime. He's got some credits coming."

So, this individual gets born into another life. Nice family, life of ease, all sorts of good things. Or if he values education, or a good career, he can have that.

But for the other person, when the Lords of Karma look in the great ledger book at the end of this lifetime, they tally it up and say, "Why, this man has some debits." And he may come back carrying a big burden on his shoulders. Other people will look at him and say, "What an unfortunate person." Yes, unfortunate, it's true. But what we fail to realize and do not want to realize, because it doesn't fit our thinking, is that a person is born the way he is for some spiritual reason.

We're all born the way we are for a certain spiritual reason.

Some say that about 95 percent of people are unhappy with the way they look. Yet the fact is, most of them chose whatever body form was available to them according to the ledger—according to the credits and debits they had earned. They're given a choice. The Lords of Karma say, "All right, you're the lucky one. Even though you've got a debit in your ledger, you can have the choice of any one of five bodies, spread out over several decades and several different cultures. What do you want?"

So you pick one. You've picked it. Of course maybe it wasn't the greatest choice on earth, but we're all creatures of our own creation.

I know these ideas are shocking to some. They'll say, "That is not so. It cannot be so." And on a purely social scale, there are people who say, "It can't be that this person was born with a disability because of some *spiritual* reason." Or let's just say it never enters their minds.

When you see someone who's carrying a burden of that sort, just remember that even the people who seem to have no burdens at all are carrying burdens of another sort. These burdens are simply called karma—cause and effect.

Now Here's the Good News

Where does this stuff come from? From ourselves. And at some point, we can wrap it up. We can be done with it and get off the wheel of reincarnation and karma.

How is this done? Somewhere along the line—meaning the line of lifetimes—the individual must find someone who can hook him up with the Voice of God. The Voice of God, in Eckankar, we call the Light and Sound of God. The two aspects of the ECK, or the Holy Spirit, are Light and Sound.

There is a way to be hooked up with them. In Eckankar, it's during the Second Initiation. This initiation comes after two years of advanced study—two years of study of the ECK monthly discourses. The Second Initiation is a landmark; it means this Soul need never return to earth again.

For many people this sounds fine. They'll say, "If I can just get away from earth and not have to come back to it ever again, I'll do whatever it takes."

Of course, there's more to the equation. There are planes above the earth plane that are still subject to karma and reincarnation. I'm speaking of the Astral, Causal, Mental, and Etheric Planes. But they're at a higher level, a finer level than the experiences on the physical plane.

In time, the earth-centered, self-centered human being will come to realize that there are people in the universe, in the physical universe, besides those on Earth. Of course, there have been reports of flying saucers for years. This is one form of life from beyond Earth. There are many different forms.

Some of the people who come from another place to Earth must use the lower vehicles of travel—spaceships. The higher spiritual beings come here by higher means, such as astral travel, for instance, or mind travel. That's another way to get around, for those who have the ability.

In Eckankar, one aspect of the teachings of the Holy Spirit is Soul Travel. It simply means the ability to travel anywhere as Soul—through the various planes, or dimensions or universes, of creation.

Astral travel only lets you travel on the Astral Plane or below, meaning the Physical

Plane. Then there's causal travel, and there's mental, or mind, travel. People who are able to do mind travel generally do it on the Mental Plane. This is the area where calculus and other higher math, the high forms of architecture, and the like come from and are developed by creative people here on earth.

Once people are able to do the higher forms of travel, they don't want to waste it flitting around earth. Generally astral travel does the job if a car, or a plane, or a train, or a bus won't.

Soul Travel and Spiritual Unfoldment

Soul Travel is one of several ways for us to experience the Light and Sound of the Holy Spirit. To draw a fine line, Soul Travel is different from the expansion of consciousness.

Soul Travel is part of the whole, while the expansion of consciousness is the whole.

Soul Travel is one way the Mahanta, the

Living ECK Master may speed up the unfoldment of an individual. Other ways include dreams, the Golden-tongued Wisdom, events in family or business life, or a spiritual realization. Yet each of these is only a part of the expansion of consciousness.

Life carries all people and beings onward to the expansion of consciousness.

For those outside of ECK, life is usually a winding road lined with blind alleys. This route to God, the Wheel of the Eighty-Four—the cycles of karma and reincarnation—is a slow journey due to Soul's many lives in the lower universes. The Physical, Astral, Causal, and Mental Planes are the rooms where Soul toils in God's school.

The HU Song

Experiences in the Sound and Light of God, however, accelerate Soul's unfoldment. The HU song, singing this holy name for God, sets these spiritual experiences into motion.

HU is pronounced like the word *hue* and is sung quietly to yourself or aloud in a long, drawn-out breath: HU-U-U-U.

Some people then find a better recall of their dreams, while the Mahanta lifts others directly into the heavens by Soul Travel. Each experience expands their consciousness.

A Spiritual Exercise to Learn about Past Lives

Sometimes there's a strong bond between people and their pets, or a bond with certain other people. And we wonder, *Why such a strong bond?*

Often the answer lies in a past life.

If we had the ability—through a dream experience, Soul Travel, or the intuitive powers of Soul—to understand this connection between that other Soul and ourselves, it would clear up so many things. It would let us treat other people with more love and kindness, because we'd have an insight into our relationship with them.

The inner worlds are as real as this outer physical world. There's a connection between the two. Sometimes if things aren't working right out here, instead of going through years of karma and trouble, you can get things back on track if you know how to go to your inner worlds.

As a spiritual exercise, before going to sleep sing *HU*, the love song to God, a few times. Then ask the Mahanta to take you to the inner worlds for an experience where you either gain the insight to change conditions or to improve yourself. Keep a pen and notepad at your bedside to write down any insights when you awaken.

Sometimes this is all that's required to help things work better in the physical world.

PAST-LIFE RESEARCH TIPS

$\mathcal{T}$o awaken past-life dreams, make a list of people and things you like or dislike. Also note if you feel a special attraction to some country, locale, or time period in history. There is a reason for such interest.

Now pay attention to your dreams.

Travel Benefits

As you travel to new places, dreams may reveal some past lives you spent there. Such dreams shed light on habits, likes, or fears. They show things gained or lost ages ago. Travel is thus a chance to revisit the foundation of what helped make you who and what you are today.

So take a trip and be aware.

A Word before You Sleep

If you want a look at your past lives, the word to sing for a few minutes at bedtime is *Mana* (say MAH-nah). Then go to sleep as usual. This word attunes you with the Causal Plane, the region of past-life memories. Remembering past lives takes practice. But others do it, and so can you.

Getting Past-Life Clues from Dreams

One night, Amy saw a blue light, bright squares of white light, and twelve ships in a dream. Some of the ships were sinking. She seemed to be up in the sky, as if in an airplane, looking down at these ships.

A month later, she saw bright squares again. This time she noticed they were like minimovies. Each one of these squares was a superbright white light. She heard the roar of engines, and in front of her she saw a panel of airplane instruments. She said, "What's going on here? Probably just another puzzling dream."

The third month, she saw a boy running through a wheat field, and overhead there was a flock of migrating Canada geese. He was trying to stay ahead of them, just running. Another puzzling dream.

Then she had a realization. The first three dreams with clear scenes all came the night after she read her monthly ECK discourse, received when she became a member of Eckankar. Each discourse has a vibration and a rhythm. It fits you at that time.

The fourth month, in a dream Amy saw a line of soldiers on horseback. These warriors were getting ready to attack an enemy. The scene again was filled with a background of bright white light, the white light from this little square where it started. She fell down into the little square. It was a very vivid experience.

After receiving a discourse on karma and reincarnation, she realized the dreams of the four previous months were playbacks of past lives.

The ocean ships, some of them sinking, and then the instrument panel in front of her, meant she was a pilot in World War II with the Royal Canadian Air Force. She knew this. She even knew her name. In the third scene she saw herself as a little boy in that lifetime. As a little boy, she wanted nothing more than to fly faster than a bird. So she fulfilled this dream of her childhood and became a pilot.

The fourth scene was from an even earlier lifetime, where she had been a warrior. She realized that in each of these two lives—as a pilot and as a warrior—she had harmed people. The reason she was back in this present lifetime was because of those and other past lives.

She remembered her name as the pilot, and after a series of coincidences, plus some research with some of the government offices in Canada, she learned more about him. One day she went to Saskatchewan, to the little town where she grew up as that pilot in the previous lifetime. She found the town very easily. She found the homestead. The wheat field was just as she remembered it. She looked at the same wide-open clear sky and the migrating birds. The homestead was right in the path of the migrating birds.

She decided she would go out to the cemetery to visit the graves of her parents from before. She knew right where the cemetery was—out of sight of town. She went there and found the grave site of her previous folks. It came to her that, as a young aviator in the Royal Canadian Air Force, this man had promised his mother to come home again. He never had. So in this lifetime as Amy, she had come back. She put flowers on the grave.

This chapter of her life began to make sense; the dreams had a physical verification. She could check things out, and she did.

SPIRITUAL EXERCISES TO WORK OFF KARMA

*W*hen an individual Soul receives the Second Initiation in Eckankar, his or her karma is taken over by the Mahanta, the Living ECK Master and given back to the individual to work off in an orderly, forward-moving manner.

Sometimes the karma works off in the dream state or in some other way. For instance, people have car accidents in the dream state instead of having to go through them out here. There are other cases where people have the accident out here, but they are miraculously saved from very severe problems. But we're not saying the teachings of ECK are a panacea for all ills. They are not. You are facing yourself.

Sometimes there are more serious things that we must face—not only to pay off a past debt, but also to grow spiritually.

These debts are never fed to the individual out of malice or spite, as if to say, "You did a bad thing, and now you must pay." The Lords of Karma do that; that is under another system. When Soul enters the path of ECK, the Lords of Karma stand to the side, and the spiritual affairs of the individual Soul come under the Mahanta. You can shortcut many of the problems. And the way you shortcut them is through the Spiritual Exercises of ECK.

You make a conscious effort to align yourself or put yourself in tune with Divine Spirit. And you do that by chanting a spiritual word, such as *HU*.

How to Avoid Daily Karma

As karma surfaces, it works out through

the weakest point in our body. As quickly as we can release our attachment to whatever is hurting us, the karma can pass off. This way we stay balanced.

Here is a technique to make less daily karma.

First, don't underestimate the importance of words in everyday speech. Comparative words such as *almost*, *nearly*, and *pretty near* used too often make us seem indecisive to the people we live and work with. Substitute more direct speech.

The overuse of demanding words such as *should*, *ought*, and *must* belong in the vocabulary of a person who desires control over others. People sense that and shy away from him. That aversion is karma.

Practice recasting your sentences along simpler, more direct lines. You can do this as a spiritual exercise to avoid making more karma.

But such modifications as better word

selection are really cosmetic changes. Daily karma is resolved best through this one simple change:

Say and do everything in the name of God, the ECK (Holy Spirit), or the Mahanta. Then your life will begin to turn around for good.

Three-Step Spiritual Exercise

Here's an exercise to help you realize that you make your own happiness; that God's love is always with you; and that change is an opportunity to grow spiritually.

Step 1. For one day, practice doing everything, large or small, for God alone. Do everything for love, for God is love. That means do it with love, joy, and thoroughness. How does this change your outlook on life? What opportunities does it bring you? Record your insights in a journal.

Step 2. Write down three key turning points or changes in your life. Note how old you were, how you responded to each change, and what you learned from it. You could make a four-column grid like this in your journal:

Turning point or change	My age	My response	What I learned
1			
2			
3			

Step 3. Contemplate this: Since change is an opportunity to grow spiritually, what change would you like to make in your life now? Write down your answer in your journal.

How to Avoid Unconscious Karma

People can also create karma in the dream state. Yet most are unaware that they do so, even as they are unaware of karma they make every day.

Each of us is like a power station. We generate energy all the time, energy that can either build or destroy. If we let unworthy thoughts or desires leave our power station, they pollute everything around us. That is bad karma. Our mind is like a machine, able to issue contaminants around the clock. Our thoughts even run on automatic at night, when we may unconsciously try to control others or harm them in the dream state.

The problem is a lack of spiritual self-discipline.

To avoid making karma, while either awake or asleep, sing the word *HU*. You can do this quietly within yourself or out loud. It's an ancient name for God. Sing it when you are angry, frightened, or alone. HU calms and restores, because it sets your thoughts upon the highest spiritual ideal.

People from any walk of life can sing *HU* for spiritual upliftment.

Questions and Answers

$\mathscr{A}$s spiritual leader of Eckankar, I get thousands of letters from seekers of truth around the world. All want direct and useful answers about how to travel the road to God. I reply personally to many of these letters.

Here are several questions I've been asked about karma and reincarnation.

Read on for clues that might help you.

The Truth about Reincarnation

People reincarnate to resolve karma created in past lifetimes. But, observing world events, it seems people are creating more karma for themselves. Will people learn to work together while resolving their karma? If we take responsibility for our actions, then when will our karma be finished so reincarnation is no longer necessary?

The whole process of refining Souls through resolving karma made in past lives is a slow, careful one. The mills of karma grind slowly, but exceedingly fine.

Yes, people are very busy every day creating new karma for themselves. The reason is they overreact to every slight. They show a lack of respect first for themselves, then for others. They need still to develop the quality of grace. Grace and respect are two signs of a mature spiritual individual, whatever his religion or beliefs.

Karma works itself off by levels through the hard experiences of life, the university of hard knocks. A Soul that completes a certain level of purification then graduates to a higher level of choice, experience, and service.

You'll find that many leaders in politics

belong to the school of adolescent Souls. It explains their shortsighted and irresponsible behavior as the supposed representatives of their electorate. But they too will someday move above their own limitations.

For a better understanding about the workings of karma, read Dr. Michael Newton's book *Journey of Souls* (Llewellyn Worldwide, Woodbury, Minnesota). The knowledge in it should give you a greater degree of contentment.

Déjà Vu

I would like to know the meaning of déjà vu. Recently, I have quite often been struck by pictures or remembrances of things I have already seen or lived. Could it be that I dreamed my entire life before?

Déjà vu is a strong feeling of already having experienced something before.

Life is a dream from beginning to end. Some people, like you, have the unusual ability of bringing the memory of a dream into the present moment. That is the reason so many things are already familiar to you. A knowledge of past lives may also open to you by way of dreams or déjà vu. Or you may catch a glimpse of future events.

Awakening Your Past-Life Memories

I would like to see my past lives. How do I go about this?

It is easiest to trace past lives through a study of your dreams.

To awaken such past-life dreams, make a note of things you greatly like or dislike. Do that also with people. Then watch your dreams. Also note if a certain country or century attracts you. There is a reason.

When we practice the Spiritual Exercises of ECK faithfully, the Inner Master will open us up to those things that are important to see regarding past lives.

Most of them need not concern us. No matter what we were in the past during any other life, we are spiritually greater today.

The wealth and position we enjoyed in past lives mean nothing unless we know how to lift ourselves from materialism into the higher worlds. This does not mean to shun the good things of this life—family, home, wealth. God loves the rich man as much as the poor. We get no special benefits if we fall for the negative tricks of asceticism or unusual austerities.

We live the spiritual life beginning where we are today. We look to see the hand of Divine Spirit guiding us toward the greater consciousness, which leads us to becoming a more direct vehicle for Spirit.

Healing Your Past Lives in Dreams

Why do we have bad dreams?

A good dream is one that helps you

grow stronger, wiser, and more full of love.

So what are bad dreams for?

Children often have nightmares until the age of six or eight, and sometimes longer. Grown-ups do too, though not so often as a rule. But why bad dreams for good people?

A bad dream is generally a memory of a past life.

It may include experiences of mistreatment, suffering, and even death. Some of us even have dreams of being born, which can give a feeling of suffocation.

These experiences are part of everyone. Children still remember bits and pieces of past lives, and these bad dreams are a part of them.

Bad dreams are old fears.

Having a bad dream is like airing out a musty room in spring. You need to face that old fear until it loses its grip, for only then can you be free to live this life to its fullest.

So good and bad dreams both hold spiritual lessons.

Dreams Prepare Us for the Future

In a recent dream I saw a situation which I understood to be a possibility in my future. Although I would eventually welcome it, I know that I am not ready for such a big step now. So I wonder why this would reveal itself to me at this time.

Dreams prepare us for the possibilities of our future. A young girl may dream of becoming a wife years before she's ready for such a role. Later, her ideas may swing away from her youthful dreams of marriage, and new ones replace them.

But when the time comes for marriage, she is ready. She is ready to step into the role of a marriage partner with more love and confidence than she would have had as a girl. This is so because of her dreams.

Our dreams simply prepare us for many

future possibilities. We can then decide which future path we want to go for.

ALWAYS REMEMBER THIS

*A*ll the lives you have ever lived were for the polishing of Soul. Like it or not, you are now at a higher and more spiritual level than in any prior incarnation. So look at yourself. Do you like what you see? Keep in mind, whatever it is, for better or worse, it's of your own making.

You are the sum of all your thoughts, feelings, and actions from this life and every lifetime in the past. Are the ECK teachings for you? Only your heart can say. Whether or not the hour and season are right for you to set foot to the most grand adventure in life, I am sure that you will never again be the same. Soul has heard the call and is yearning to go home.

To find love and spiritual freedom—that's the purpose of our incarnations.

Good dreams to you, and many happy journeys.

NEXT STEPS IN
SPIRITUAL EXPLORATION

- **Try a spiritual exercise.**
  Review the spiritual exercises in this book or on our Web site.
  Experiment with them.

- **Browse our Web site: www.Eckankar.org.**
  Watch videos; get free books, answers to FAQs, and more info.

- **Attend an Eckankar event in your area.**
  Visit "Eckankar around the World" on our Web site.

- **Read additional books** about the ECK teachings.

- **Explore advanced spiritual study** with the Eckankar discourses that come with membership.

- **Call or write to us:** Call 1-800-LOVE GOD (1-800-568-3463, toll-free, automated) or (952) 380-2200 (direct).

- Write to: ECKANKAR, Dept. BK88, PO Box 2000, Chanhassen, MN 55317-2000 USA.

FOR FURTHER READING
By Harold Klemp

ECK Wisdom on Conquering Fear

Would having more courage and confidence help you make the most of this lifetime?

Going far beyond typical self-help advice, this book invites you to explore divine love as the antidote to anxiety and the doorway to inner freedom.

You will discover ways to identify the karmic roots of fear and align with your highest ideals.

Use this book to soar beyond your limitations and reap the benefits of self-mastery.

Live life to its fullest potential!

ECK Wisdom on Dreams

This dream study will help you be more *awake* than you've ever been!

ECK Wisdom on Dreams reveals the most ancient of dream teachings for a richer and more productive life today.

In this dynamic book, author Harold Klemp shows you how to remember your dreams, apply dream wisdom to everyday situations, recognize prophetic dreams, and more.

You will be introduced to the art of dream interpretation and offered techniques to discover the treasures of your inner worlds.

Spiritual Wisdom on Health and Healing

This booklet is rich with spiritual keys to better health on every level.

Discover the spiritual roots of illness and how gratitude can open your heart to God's love and healing.

Simple spiritual exercises go deep to help you get personal divine guidance and insights.

Revitalize your connection with the true healing power of God's love.

ECK Wisdom on Inner Guidance

Looking for answers, guidance, protection?

Help can come as a nudge, a dream, a vision, or a quiet voice within you. This book offers new ways to connect with the ever-present guidance of ECK, the Holy Spirit. Start today!

Discover how to listen to the Voice of God; attune to your true self; work with an inner guide; benefit from dreams, waking dreams, and Golden-tongued Wisdom; and ignite your creativity to solve problems.

Each story, technique, and spiritual exercise is a doorway to greater confidence and love for life.

Open your heart and let God's voice speak to you!

ECK Wisdom on Life after Death

All that lies ahead is already within your heart.

ECK Wisdom on Life after Death invites you to explore the eternal nature of you!

Author Harold Klemp offers you new perspectives on seeing heaven before you die, meeting with departed loved ones, near-death experiences, getting help from spiritual guides, animals in heaven, and dealing with grief.

Try the techniques and spiritual exercise included in this book to find answers and explore the secrets of life after death—for yourself.

Spiritual Wisdom on Prayer, Meditation, and Contemplation

Bring balance and wonder to your life!

This booklet is a portal to your direct, personal connection with Divine Spirit.

Harold Klemp shows how you can experience the powerful benefits of contemplation—"a conversation with the most secret, most

 genuine, and most mysterious part of yourself."

Move beyond traditional meditation via dynamic spiritual exercises. Learn about the uplifting chant of HU (an ancient holy name for God), visualization, creative imagination, and other active techniques.

Spiritual Wisdom on Relationships

Find the answers to common questions of the heart, including the truth about Soul mates, how to strengthen a marriage, and how to know if a partnership is worth developing.

The spiritual exercises included in this booklet can help you break a pattern of poor relationships and find balance. You'll learn new ways to open your heart to love and enrich your relationship with God.

This booklet is a key for anyone wanting more love to give, more love to get. It's a key to better relationships with everyone in your life.

ECK Wisdom on Solving Problems

Problems? Problems! Why do we have so many? What causes them? Can we avoid them?

Author Harold Klemp, the spiritual leader of Eckankar, can help you answer these questions and more. His sense of humor and practical approach offer spiritual keys to unlock the secrets to effective problem solving.

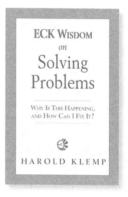

Learn creative, time-tested techniques to

- Find the root cause of a problem
- Change your viewpoint and overcome difficulties
- Conquer your fears
- Work beyond symptoms to solutions
- Kindle your creativity
- Master your karma, past and present
- Receive spiritual guidance that can transform the way you see yourself and your life

The Call of Soul

Discover how to find spiritual freedom in this lifetime and the infinite world of God's love for you. Includes a CD with dream and Soul Travel techniques.

HU, the Most Beautiful Prayer

Singing *HU*, the ancient name for God, can open your heart and lead you to a new understanding of yourself. Includes a CD of the HU song.

Past Lives, Dreams, and Soul Travel

These stories and exercises help you find your true purpose, discover greater love than you've ever known, and learn that spiritual freedom is within reach.

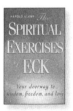

The Spiritual Exercises of ECK

This book is a staircase with 131 steps leading to the doorway to spiritual freedom, self-mastery, wisdom, and love. A comprehensive volume of spiritual exercises for every need.

81

The Road to Spiritual Freedom, Mahanta Transcripts, Book 17

Sri Harold's wisdom and heart-opening stories of everyday people having extraordinary experiences tell of a secret truth at work in *your* life—there is divine purpose and meaning to every experience you have.

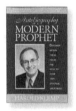

How to Survive Spiritually in Our Times, Mahanta Transcripts, Book 16

Discover how to reinvent yourself spiritually—to thrive in a changing world. Stories, tools, techniques, and spiritual insights to apply in your life now.

Autobiography of a Modern Prophet

This riveting story of Harold Klemp's climb up the Mountain of God will help you discover the keys to your own spiritual greatness.

Those Wonderful ECK Masters

Would you like to have *personal* experience with spiritual masters that people all over the world—since the beginning of time—have looked to for guidance, protection, and divine love? This book includes real-life stories and spiritual exercises to meet eleven ECK Masters.

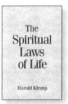

The Spiritual Laws of Life

Learn how to keep in tune with your true spiritual nature. Spiritual laws reveal the behind-the-scenes forces at work in your daily life.

Available at bookstores, from online booksellers, or directly from Eckankar: www.ECKBooks.org; (952) 380-2200; ECKANKAR, Dept. BK88, PO Box 2000, Chanhassen, MN 55317-2000 USA.

GLOSSARY

Words set in SMALL CAPS are defined elsewhere in this glossary.

Blue Light How the MAHANTA often appears in the inner worlds to the CHELA or seeker.

chela A spiritual student. Often a member of ECKANKAR.

ECK The Life Force, the Holy Spirit, or Audible Life Current which sustains all life.

Eckankar *EHK-ahn-kahr* The Path of Spiritual Freedom. Also known as the Ancient Science of SOUL TRAVEL. A truly spiritual way of life for the individual in modern times. The teachings provide a framework for anyone to explore their own spiritual experiences. Established by Paul Twitchell, the modern-day founder, in 1965. The word means Co-worker with God.

ECK Masters Spiritual Masters who can assist and protect people in their spiritual studies and travels. The ECK Masters are from a long line of God-Realized SOULS who know the responsibility that goes with spiritual freedom.

God-Realization The state of God Consciousness. Complete and conscious awareness of God.

84

HU *HYOO* The most ancient, secret name for God. The singing of the word *HU* is considered a love song to God. It can be sung aloud or silently to oneself to align with God's love.

initiation Earned by a member of ECKANKAR through spiritual unfoldment and service to God. The initiation is a private ceremony in which the individual is linked to the Sound and Light of God.

Karma, Law of The Law of Cause and Effect, action and reaction, justice, retribution, and reward, which applies to the lower or psychic worlds: the Physical, Astral, Causal, Mental, and Etheric PLANES.

Klemp, Harold The present MAHANTA, the LIVING ECK MASTER. Sri Harold Klemp became the Mahanta, the Living ECK Master in 1981. His spiritual name is Wah Z.

Living ECK Master The title of the spiritual leader of ECKANKAR. He leads SOUL back to God. He teaches in the physical world as the Outer Master, in the dream state as the Dream Master, and in the spiritual worlds as the Inner Master. SRI HAROLD KLEMP became the MAHANTA, the Living ECK Master in 1981.

Mahanta An expression of the Spirit of God that is always with you. Sometimes seen as a BLUE LIGHT or Blue Star or in the form of the Mahanta, the LIVING ECK MASTER. The highest state of God Consciousness on earth, only embodied in the Living ECK Master. He is the Living Word.

planes   Levels of existence, such as the Physical, Astral, Causal, Mental, Etheric, and Soul Planes.

Self-Realization   Soul recognition. The entering of Soul into the Soul Plane and there beholding Itself as pure Spirit. A state of seeing, knowing, and being.

Soul   The True Self, an individual, eternal spark of God. The inner, most sacred part of each person. Soul can see, know, and perceive all things. It is the creative center of Its own world.

Soul Travel   The expansion of consciousness. The ability of Soul to transcend the physical body and travel into the spiritual worlds of God. Soul Travel is taught only by the Living ECK Master. It helps people unfold spiritually and can provide proof of the existence of God and life after death.

Sound and Light of ECK   The Holy Spirit. The two aspects through which God appears in the lower worlds. People can experience them by looking and listening within themselves and through Soul Travel.

Spiritual Exercises of ECK   Daily practices for direct, personal experiences with the Sound

Current. Creative techniques using contemplation and the singing of sacred words to bring the higher awareness of S<small>OUL</small> into daily life.

Sri *SREE* A title of spiritual respect, similar to reverend or pastor, used for those who have attained the Kingdom of God. In E<small>CKANKAR</small>, it is reserved for the M<small>AHANTA</small>, the L<small>IVING</small> ECK M<small>ASTER</small>.

For more explanations of E<small>CKANKAR</small> terms, see *A Cosmic Sea of Words: The ECKANKAR Lexicon* by Harold Klemp.

ABOUT THE AUTHOR

Author Harold Klemp is known as a pioneer of today's focus on "everyday spirituality." He was raised on a Wisconsin farm and attended divinity school. He also served in the US Air Force.

In 1981, after lifetimes of training, he became the spiritual leader of Eckankar, the Path of Spiritual Freedom. His full title is Sri Harold Klemp, the Mahanta, the Living ECK Master. His mission is to help people find their way back to God in this life.

Each year, Harold Klemp speaks to many thousands of seekers at Eckankar seminars. Author of more than one hundred books, he continues to write, including many articles and spiritual-study discourses. His inspiring and practical approach to spirituality helps many thousands of people worldwide find greater freedom, wisdom, and love in their lives.